Charles Allen Oakley and the Scottish Division of the National Institute of Industrial Psychology - a Contribution to Occupational Psychology in Great Britain?

(with reference to Charles S. Myers and his original Division N.I.I.P. in London).

LORI . L. ALLAN

University of Stirling

Psychology Honours Project

March 23rd 1995

Supervisor: Dr. D. Fryer

CONTENTS

1. ACKNOWLEDGEMENTS
2. LIST OF APPENDICES
3. ABSTRACT
4. INTRODUCTION
5. METHOD
6. RESULTS: ORIGINS OF THE N.I.I.P.
7. RESULTS: OAKLEY AND THE S.D.N.I.I.P.
8. DISCUSSION
9. CONCLUSIONS
10. APPENDIX ONE
11. APPENDIX TWO

13. BIBLIOGRAPHY

LIST OF APPENDICES

APPENDIX ONE   -   Charles Oakley
                   Background information.

               -   photographs, exam papers

APPENDIX TWO   -   David Duncan
                   interview transcript.

ACKNOWLEDGEMENTS

I would like to acknowledge and thank my supervisor, David Fryer, for his help and advice in the completion of this project.

I would also like to thank:

1. Mrs. J.H. McKillop for lending the personal papers of her Father, C.A. Oakley.

2. David Duncan for allowing me to interview him.

ABSTRACT

(Lori L. Allan, Reg.no.- 910804-2, Supervisor-Dr.D.Fryer)

Little information can be found regarding the formation of the National Institute of Industrial Psychology in 1919 and the setting up of its Scottish Division in 1928. The motivation behind setting up a Scottish Division was examined as well as its proposed aims and various achievements.

To gain an insight into the real dilemmas faced by both Divisions, historical/qualitative analysis was used, and a search of archives helped clarify these issues. It was found that these Divisions had different ideals and faced different external-internal pressures.

It is suggested that the study of the N.I.I.P. and S.D.N.I.I.P. should be one of the main concerns of any researcher interested in the history of Occupational Psychology.

INTRODUCTION AND LITERATURE SURVEY

Today, occupational psychology is widely acknowledged as a respectable and valid area of research to be engaged in. Unfortunately, this has not always been the case. At the time of the emergence of this "new Industrial Psychology" during the 1914-18 War, most people will have been inclined to conjuring up a picture of the industrial psychologist taking on the role of a manipulator of workers, in order to satisfy the rapacious greed of management with its insatiable demand for profits.

The development of the National Institute of Industrial Psychology (set up in 1919 by Charles S. Myers) was about to change such attitudes if they existed and demonstrate that productivity is not a goal sought only by management and shareholders. They were to help everyone understand that our whole society depends on the efficient production of a vast range of goods for its very existence. It was to be made clear that the more efficient and plentiful is production, the more goods and services are available to society and therefore the more society as a whole is likely to benefit. The N.I.I.P. was to prove its value especially in its research on the individual in an organisation. The more efficient the productive process, the more he is likely to be rewarded and the more secure is his job likely to be.

It is very interesting to look at the development of industrial psychology in Great Britain and the N.I.I.P.'s influence on it. Obtaining such information is fairly easy. The real challenge, however, is attempting to get an 'insider's' look at the internal dynamics which took place concerning individual members of the Institute. A study of this can give us an even better idea as to what external pressures were felt by the Institute and the general attitude towards industrial psychology at the time. With some effort, one can get a fairly good idea about what was going on in Myers' Institute and the research it carried out. However, a clearer picture of its work can only be depicted with an insight into what went on in the U.K. as a whole. This can be done by looking at the Scottish Division of the National Institute of Industrial Psychology which was formed in 1928.

The interest in the S.D.N.I.I.P. increases when one considers that there are virtually no publications referring to its work. The Director of this Division was Charles Allen Oakley and there is even less information available as to what he was involved in before joining the N.I.I.P. and why he came to be director of the Scottish Division. The fact that he led this division brings one to ask the question of whether Oakley was a main contributor to British Occupational Psychology. It does strike one as rather odd that those interested in the history of occupational psychology neither took up the subject of the Scottish Division nor that of the life of Charles A. Oakley as a topic of interest. Therefore, the aim in investigating such an area in this paper will be to explore the following issues and questions: (1) How and why was the Scottish Division set up? (2) What were its aims and how did its actual achievements compare to what it wanted to achieve? (3) The relationship between Myers and Oakley (4) Oakley's role in the Scottish Division (5) How Oakley's ideas relate to recent research in occupational psychology.

LITERATURE REVIEW

When one digs deeper into the main concerns involved in these issues, one finds that there is a fair amount of literature about Myers and his Institute. Myers published quite a few books such as his <u>Industrial Psychology in Great Britain (1925)</u>, <u>Industrial Psychology (1929)</u>, and <u>Ten Years of Industrial Psychology: An Account of the First Decade of N.I.I.P, (1932)</u>. The N.I.I.P. itself had its own journals; <u>The Journal of the N.I.I.P. (1922-1931)</u>, <u>The Human Factor</u> (1932-1937) and <u>Occupational Psychology</u> (1938-1977).

Literature relating to Oakley and his Scottish Division is very scarce when one makes a quick superficial search. Myers wrote very briefly of S.D.N.I.I.P. in his <u>Ten Years of Industrial Psychology</u>. Some basic works by Oakley are easily obtainable in most libraries in Glasgow and Edinburgh. For example, Oakley wrote an autobiography entitled <u>Those Were the Years</u> (1983). He also wrote <u>Men at Work</u> (1975).

A quick glance using the BIDS information system shows that more detailed information would appear to be unpublished and stored in archives or special collections. One such source is the London Wellcome Library of Medical History. The British Library of Political and Economic Science was said to

stock the archives of the N.I.I.P. from 1919 - 1974. The
Warwick University Modern Records Centre was also listed as
possibly having some papers. From Oakley's autobiography, a
hint was given that another place to look might be the Glasgow
Chamber of Commerce as Oakley was chairman of it.

METHODOLOGY

Clearly, the best way to discover what really went on in
Myers' Institute and Charles Oakley's Scottish Division at
this point is to engage in qualitative/historical research
which involves the use of archives and secondary analysis.
It should be mentioned that the decision to use historical
documents is not one that the non-historian should take
lightly. A planned study can go through a number of changes,
which in part reflects the failure to appreciate fully certain
types of problem. For example, one might find that much of
what one intends to use is no longer available or is
"obscurely catalogued". Consequently, the general thrust of
the project may have to be reassessed and refocused. This
project is representative of some of the problems and indeed
surprises that can be encountered during research.

First of all, a search of Scottish libraries was attempted,
and came to a dead end. Glasgow Mitchell Library had copies
of work by Oakley of which the author was unaware. For
example, it was found that Oakley wrote The Last Tram (for
Glasgow Transport Department in 1962) and The Buyers' Guide to
Scottish industries; Who's who and where of 5,500
manufacturing Firms (1951). This was of little use, but

suggested that Oakley's interests were spread more widely than was at first anticipated.

The above is about all that was found of published material. The major source of information was clearly to come from unpublished archival material and this was to involve a bit of detective work in London. People who knew Oakley personally were also a potential source of information - e.g. members of Oakley's family or close friends and colleagues.

Many people were contacted by 'phone and through letters. Once contacted, the following sources proved unsuccessful:

- The National Register of Archives (Scotland).

- The Royal Society (London)

- The Royal Commission on Historical Manuscripts (London)

- The University of East London (suggested I look for a thesis at Edinburgh University which unfortunately was not there. Also, a Mr. Harbens Shahal claimed they once had the N.I.I.P. library but the contents had been dispersed).

- Glasgow Junior Chamber of Commerce (only kept records of recent organisations).

- Warwick University Modern Records Centre.

- London Wellcome Library (their collection of N.I.I.P work was uncatalogued and was sidelined as a "non-priority").

- Tim Caruthers of Glasgow University Occupational Psychology Department.

- Dr. Phil Gardiner (retired professor of Glasgow University who only had vague recollections of Oakley).

- Science Museum in London (curator Tim Boon still has not catalogued what N.I.I.P. material and equipment he has).

The above revelations were certainly demoralising, but the desired information was eventually found, although it was discovered towards of the end of the research. The first breakthrough was made with the discovery of an abundance of information in the British Library of Political and Economic Science in London. There was a vast amount of information on Myers' Division in the form of reports and letters from firms, etc. Unfortunately the only information available on the Scottish Division was a collection of Minutes from its meetings, 1930 - 1951. Valuable information was there, but it was quite clear that even some of this material had been lost. The most valuable information to be found in London was obtained through an interview with David Duncan. He knew Oakley well and became a member of N.I.I.P. in 1953. He brought the subject to life and clarified the issue of how Oakley's Scottish Division was viewed by the London Division.

More detailed information about Myers' Institute was found with the help of Dr. A. Lovie of the Department of Psychology in Liverpool. He is responsible for the British Psychological Society Archives. Journals of N.I.I.P. were found here along with more reports.

Sylvia Shimmin of Leeds University was kind enough to send me excerpts from her newly published book Fifty Years of Occupational Psychology in Britain (1994) which was useful but contained the same information as the interview with David Duncan.

Of course the most valuable information was obtained from Mrs. J.H. McKillop, Oakley's daughter. This was obtained literally at the last minute, but was the information which was initially meant to be central to my research aims. I wrote to Mrs. McKillop months ago and probably did not get a response because she was in the process of moving from her house in 10 Kirklee Circus, Glasgow. I consider myself lucky to have got hold of the materials, as Mrs. McKillop was about to hand them over to Glasgow University, where they probably would have only been left to deteriorate and remain uncatalogued.

Some of the material obtained from the above sources was at times hand-copied in pencil (archive rules) because they were too delicate to be photocopied. These consist mainly of reports and minutes from N.I.I.P. / S.D.N.I.I.P. meetings.

In the Results section, most of the information is from such a source. When selecting information from Oakley's 1993 writings, I included in the Results section whatever I could manage to decipher. Whole pages were unfortunately missing from some of Oakley's accounts and because he was writing them in the last year of his life, his writing is in many cases blurred and illegible. Also, these were all written in fountain pen which does not generally stand up to the test of time so it is just as well these documents are being looked at now (see catalogue in appendix). Hopefully the following account will prove useful and interesting as most of the documents used are personal and portray the issues at hand vividly.

RESULTS

THE ORIGINS

According to Michael Rose (1975), the history of Industrial Psychology began during the 1914-1918 War, when Munsterburg's <u>Psychology in Industrial Efficiency</u> was first translated into English. Munsterburg brought to America experimental techniques learned in Europe. This eventually inspired the work of Bernard Muscio. Myers himself records (1942) that it was Muscio's book <u>Lectures on Industrial Psychology</u>, delivered in Sydney in 1916, and published the following year, which finally convinced him of the practicality and indeed the necessity to set up an independent institute for the furtherance of this new 'Industrial Psychology'. As early as April 1919 Myers and Welch had instituted an organising committee for an <u>Institute for Industrial Psychology</u>.

As Frisby (1970) puts it,

"The effective growth of industrial psychology depends on the acceptance it can gain from those who are the subjects of its enquiries and those who provide the material resources it must have".

Myers and Welch were clearly aware of this - and the possible implications of ignoring it. Thus the organising committee set about discussing its plans with organised labour, philanthropic institutions and the business community. The committee also appealed to

"Heads of Departments in Universities and other Institutions throughout the Kingdom who were most interested in the practical application of Psychology and Physiology, for their co-operation in the work of the Institute" (Journal of the N.I.I.P. 1922).

All these approaches were successful. In 1919 promises of support were received from "Cadbury Bros., Messrs. Pascall, Messrs. Rowntree, Tootal Broadhurst Lee Co. and a number of other firms" (ibid). The Carnegie U.K. Trust also granted the N.I.I.P. £1,000 for its first five years. The initial scientific committee of the N.I.I.P. met on December 11th 1921. The N.I.I.P. had managed to enrol some 25 leading academics. They included Bartlett, Burt, Drever, Edgell, Farmer, Muscio, Pear, Spearman, Valentine and of course Myers who chaired the Scientific Committee which gave the N.I.I.P. an extraordinarily able and experienced advisory body to oversee its work throughout the ensuing years.

The earliest organising expenses had been met by Myers, Welch, Mr. George Croll and the Bradford Dyers Association. Fuller accounts of these earliest days are available in the N.I.I.P.'s own journal (pp.2-8 1922 and Frisby pp.35-50, 1970).

Myers was in effective control of the N.I.I.P. in its earliest years as its full time Director. Thus as we shall see its early work conforms to Myers' conception of the N.I.I.P. as a sort of industrial teaching hospital. He wrote in 1942 "Indeed the N.I.I.P. was, in my mind to fulfil the functions of a hospital viz teaching, practice and research".

Myers' emphasis on service and research (often combined) in the field led to the accumulation of an immense amount of data. The sheer volume, diversity and pioneering nature of the N.I.I.P.'s work before the War is astonishing (see appendix).

SETTING UP THE SCOTTISH DIVISION

"The Scottish Division was very much Charles Oakley's foundation and essentially, once he had established it, they just left him alone".

This is the opinion of David Duncan as to the relationship between the London Division and the Scottish Division of the N.I.I.P. The issues involved are complex as to why Oakley was left to act on his own initiative. One answer to this can be found when we look at the relationship between Oakley and C.S. Myers.

In Welch and Myers' book Ten Years of Industrial Psychology there is no indication of any tension between these bodies. It is explained quite matter of factly that in 1928 C.S. Myers, who had founded the N.I.I.P. some years before, addressed meetings of businessmen in the larger manufacturing centres including Glasgow. He had previously created the Psychological Laboratory at Cambridge University, and his aim was to have lectureships in industrial psychology established in several British universities.

The best response came in Glasgow, and the Chamber of Commerce appointed a fund-raising Committee. According to a confidential document from the Chamber of Commerce, (1929) this committee was to include Sam Mavor (chairman), John Urie of City Bakeries (vice-chairman), Sir George Mitchell, the

Lanarkshire coal-owner, Sir John Mann, C.A., John Drysdale of Drysdale and Company, Gordon Daly of Daly's, Neil J. MacLean of Barr and Stroud, and Norman Duthie, C.A. The President of the Chamber, Mr. S.R. Beale made the motion that a Scottish Division should be formed. He made a statement that a Scottish Division of the N.I.I.P. be established in Glasgow and associated with a Lectureship at Glasgow University as part of the Department of Political Economy. The Constitution of the Scottish Division was then approved by the Directors of the Chamber. This agreement provided "inter-alia" for (1) a Lectureship in Industrial Psychology in the Department of Political Economy in the University of Glasgow; (2) the extension in Scotland of the work of the Institute in the Industrial and Commercial spheres; (3) Vocational Guidance to young people on leaving school, and vocational selection for specific occupations.

Charles Oakley (1993) wrote briefly about his role in this new division. He mentions that he lectured part-time at the University and was to give all his lectures on Mondays and Fridays, so keeping himself free for other duties on Tuesdays, Wednesdays and Thursdays, and also on Saturday mornings, which were considered particularly suitable for giving vocational guidance. He describes how when he was Scottish Divisional Director of the N.I.I.P. he was to have his office in town, not in the University. He says this was because Sam Mavor and several of his fellow committee members were governors of the Royal Technical College and described Gilmorehill as an 'ivory tower'. He says accommodation was finally found for him in a vacant room in a central city office, a typist secretary was engaged for him and a brass plate was added to the office on the doorway saying "Scottish Office - National Institute of Industrial Psychology". According to Oakley, it was expected that the formation of the Division would lead to the N.I.I.P. procuring assignments in Scottish factories (he believed the N.I.I.P. was accepted as the precursor of the management consultancy firms). Getting the assignments was to be Oakley's responsibility as Divisional Director but they were to be undertaken by investigators from the N.I.I.P.'s headquarters staff.

This last aspect is interesting because minutes from the Scottish Division reveal a strong resistance on the part of the National Executive against Oakley doing his own factory investigations. This minute is from a 1932 meeting (8th October). It was stated that Mr. Oakley is not to be expected to supervise surveys or "investigations"'. From this statement, it would seem that the National Executive was trying to imply that Oakley didn't have time for these things and should not be approached regarding such matters. It was also stated in this minute that 'Mr. Oakley is to acquire experience in London as practicable "to help him in getting investigations and in conversing with employers"'.
In the course of this discussion Dr. Miles explained that in his view Oakley was not in a position to collaborate on investigations, that in technical matters supervision must come from London. The view of the meeting was that Oakley should be put in a position to enable him to keep in touch

with the work being done by the Investigator so that he could discuss any matters which clients might raise. It was agreed that on technical matters the decision must be with London. It could be a misinterpretation on the author's part as to the nature of the relationship between Oakley and the Division in London. One could say that they were simply trying to facilitate Oakley's role as both lecturer of Industrial Psychology and Divisional Director of the Scottish branch of the N.I.I.P. However, David Duncan had also read this minute and agreed it "implied that they were a bit doubtful about Charles and his ability to carry out an investigation unsupervised".

Perhaps this was no surprise to Oakley, as it was written in the Constitution of the Scottish Division:

The National Executive will <u>assist</u> the Scottish Division by nominating, as occasions require trained and selected members of its own staff as permanently resident assistants to the Divisional Director for the purpose of carrying out investigations or rendering other technical services, or doing research work in Scotland".

Given this piece of information, it would seem that the London Division viewed this as a matter of 'assistance' to the Scottish Division - not a comment on Oakley's abilities as an investigator. With so little evidence we can only speculate on this matter. Perhaps Oakley even appreciated their help, although as we shall see he did not receive such help when he needed it the most. There are hints of bitterness in his 1993 writings which are negative comments about Myers and the N.I.I.P. As was mentioned before, these scraps and notes were written in his last year of life and are almost illegible

- but when looked at carefully, they reveal a very personal account of what Oakley was thinking at the time.

Oakley wrote one section, or reminiscence of his University Lectures which was entitled 'Preparing my Lectures'. In it, he tells us there was one aspect of his delivering lectures in Industrial Psychology to university students that no one had discovered. He reveals that he had never given a lecture on Industrial Psychology in his life. He observes how neither Dr. Myers nor anyone else had ever taught on this rather crucial matter. Oakley says that all along he had assumed that Myers had the matter in hand and he believed this was probably his intention but Myers failed to do so. It struck Oakley as incredible that he was so 'remiss'. Oakley goes on to say that Myers asked him to commit himself to a whole University Session and be faced with such headings as Vocational Guidance, Industrial Training, Fatigue Study and so on without giving him the 'slightest idea' about where he could get any information about them. The best clue to Oakley's feelings about the staff of the N.I.I.P. is when he next states:

"Actually what I did after I realised that I was not going to get the slightest help from him (<u>or from anyone else on the Institute's Staff</u>), was to turn once more to Glasgow's Mitchell Library - not as I did in the past to its Glasgow Department but to its Technical Section, and I approached it to read some of its books and papers dealing with it".

Lastly, Oakley mentions that as he had no books to recommend to his classes for reading he handed over before each lecture a typed paper giving the headings with a section or two on each topic (A few copies of these 'typed papers' have been found and will be discussed later on).

Certainly, it was surprising that Oakley was still writing about these issues during the last year of his life and we can only conclude that he felt very strongly about them. We can understand why Oakley was annoyed when we consider that one of Myers' reasons for setting up a Scottish Division was to have lectureships in Industrial Psychology established in universities across Great Britain. If we look at it from Oakley's point of view, Myers should have had a clear syllabus in mind for the teachers of these courses if establishing Lectureships was one of his goals. David Duncan gives us another clue as to why Oakley was dissatisfied with his colleagues down south. Duncan says the Lectureship in Industrial Psychology did not provide enough money for Oakley to make a living and so "Charles Oakley rather took against what he regarded as the 'Cambridge Mafia'". In other words, the characteristic of Cambridge Graduates such as Myers and Bartlett was that at the time most of them came from rich families. Duncan points out that Oakley was completely different from them in this respect, as his Father was a Naval Architect. This suggests that Oakley's way of thinking clearly differed from that of the Cambridge School.

There are several good examples of how Oakley's ideas differed from those of the London Division. Duncan suggests that

Oakley must have had more experience of accident prevention for example, because he was working in heavy industry where accidents were most likely to occur. In fact, Oakley wrote two papers on the phenomenon of accidents in Industry - one on factors leading to accident causation and the other dealing with accident prevention. Another point that Duncan makes is that the Institute was not involved in much research on the subject of unemployment. According to him, Oakley was living in the centre of a depressed area in which industries were depressed. For this reason, his paper "Some Psychological Problems of a Depressed area" (1936) is a very realistic portrayal of the psychological effects of unemployment. His experience of serving an Apprenticeship in a Clyde shipyard at the time the shipbuilding industry collapsed (1923) was crucial, as he was able to listen to his fellow apprentices concerning their experience of unemployment. In Oakley's words;

"They have led me to favour the opinion that the problem is largely summed up in the term 'self respect'. I have never met an unemployed man who did not really want to work. Those persons who say otherwise have, in my opinion, failed to understand the behaviour of the unemployed men to whom they have spoken. (pp.393).

From this quote, we can understand that Oakley had a very down to earth approach and he identified with the people he wrote about. This approach was probably very different to that of his colleagues down south. As Duncan says "There was really a difference in atmosphere and a difference in emphasis".

Turning back again to the subject of the setting up of the Scottish Division, Oakley's 1993 writings are really all that remain for those wanting to find out <u>why</u> it was established and why Oakley was chosen. Again, it is important to remember Duncan's opinion that once the Scottish Division was established, Oakley was 'very much an operator on his own'., because the north was 'heavily unionised', whereas most of the studies and investigations carried out by the N.I.I.P. London Division were done mostly in 'non-unionised firms employing women'. Oakley's division, as Duncan points out, was working mainly in heavy engineering in firms which employed men. Thus Duncan's opinion that: 'the people who came north didn't really fit that scene at all - and so Oakley kept very much to himself'.

Apparently, Oakley (1993) was of the same opinion. In a section entitled ' My Three Meetings with Dr. Charles Myers' Oakley describes his three meetings at the Institute in Central London in the Spring of 1929. Again it is difficult to read, but basically, he said the first meeting followed the 'outright rejection' by the Glasgow Committee under Sam Mavor's chairmanship of the two men put forward by Myers as his choice for the Glasgow Appointment. The Glasgow Committee had rejected both as unlikely to get on well with Scottish workpeople. Oakley says he did not know who they were and that they were not from the Institute's staff but his guess was that both were members of Cambridge University staff and had been associated with him there. An interesting revelation by Oakley in this section is the following:

I also surmise that .. [undecipherable] also disapproved of Dr. Myers' choice and that there had been a dispute at the Institute's headquarters about it.

This statement suggests that Oakley was not actually Myers' first choice for the position of Divisional Director. As David Duncan believed, the formation of this division was more a result of pressure from Oakley and the decision was made by Sam Mavor. Oakley describes the action taken by Sam Mavor. He says that Mavor had consulted a Professor John Cormack to see if he had any suggestions. He goes on to say that it was his good luck that he had been to see this professor about the delay in completing the Glasgow Corporation's College of Engineering for which he was backing Oakley. This professor said he was willing to nominate Charles Oakley for the Lectureship at the University in Industrial Psychology. Sam Mavor's own committee then interviewed Oakley. He remembered that what impressed him the most was that he had served a six-year apprenticeship at John Brown's shipyard. He then adds (perhaps with some pride): 'I was so utterly different from the two men Dr. Myers had sent them'.

It is not known if there is more to this document or not, but it certainly solved the mystery as to why it was Oakley who was chosen for this post. It would seem that Sam Mavor and Professor John Cormack shared Oakley's view that Cambridge staff could not understand the climate in Scotland would not have been able to identify with the issues facing Scottish Industry at the time. Although Oakley's writings have been difficult to decipher, this piece must have been interpreted correctly, because J.D. Cormack's name appears in the 1929

Glasgow Chamber of Commerce meeting under the heading: 'Formation of Scottish Committee'. It makes even more sense when we consider that at this point, no decision had been made about who should fill the position of Divisional Director. At this time it was only decided that the position should be associated with a Lectureship at the University.

Another interesting note left by Oakley is a section he entitled 'My bizarre first day at the Institute'. The fact that he wrote so much about it (especially in his last year of life), shows that he took a real interest in the Institute's activities. In this section, Oakley says that once everything was settled he contacted Dr. Myers and it was agreed that he should report the following Monday morning at the London Institute. When he arrived, however, he was met by Myers' two personal assistants, Gladys .. [undecipherable] and Christopher Scarborough - both of whom later became close friends of Oakley and they said with 'considerable embarrassment' that he had accepted to spend a week in a country house. He had just told them to introduce Oakley to Dr. Miles, the Deputy Director, but he had gone to the North of England for the week visiting factories.

Oakley then met Miss Miles, his secretary (who turned out to be Myers' sister) and she said he was to spend the week in the Institute's library. At that stage he pointed out that he had just come down from two universities both of which had more material than he supposed the Institute had. He said he would look at some of the Institute's reports on investigations it had carried out.   She replied that the reports were locked in a cupboard to which she had the key and only opened it with Dr. Miles' authority.

Not surprisingly, Oakley goes on to say "I was on the point of ending my short career as an industrial psychologist".   He was then told to see another secretary, who explained that Dr. Miles and Myers were at loggerheads.   Dr. Myers had gone to Birmingham and Glasgow almost entirely on his own initiative and had assured Dr. Miles he would be consulted.   There is one more sentence that is illegible.   However, from this much, we can understand that Oakley's first day at the Institute was far from pleasant and indeed, it is surprising he choose to do work for them in Scotland.

OAKLEY'S LECTURESHIP:

Evidence of Oakley's work at Glasgow University appears in his lecturing notebook (see catalogue) and in exam papers he devised for his classes.   The exam papers date from 1931 - 1971 and cover such topics as Fatigue Study and Working Conditions, Environmental Engineering, Prevention of Accidents (safety engineering), the Art of Management, and Vocational Guidance.   Oakley also gave lectures on these topics at Heriot-Watt, thirteen lectures at Paisley Technical College, a short series of lectures at the Royal Technical College, a summer-school course on Vocational Guidance for the National Committee for the Training of Teachers in 1938 and interestingly, some lectures on Advertising Psychology at the Glasgow and West of Scotland Commercial College, but there is no information about these particular lectures in Oakley's notebook.

In this section, we will discuss how relevant Oakley's lectures were to what is being taught in occupational psychology today. This will include some discussion of Oakley's unpublished work, Industrial Psychology (1962) which was written after Oakley's Men at Work (1945) and according to his daughter, Mrs. McKillop, was used as an outline for his lectures.

FATIGUE STUDY AND WORKING CONDITIONS:

On this topic, Oakley lectured about such factors as length of the working year, length of the working week, distribution during the working day (ie. shift working and authorised rest pauses), time rates, financial stimulants, profit sharing, and measuring work (how much has been done). Oakley wrote about these exact topics in his unpublished work (1962) under a section entitled 'Fatigue and Willingness to Work'. Essentially, much of what Oakley wrote about still applies to modern research on fatigue study. This is especially true when we look at shift-working. As Oakley wrote:

"The night shift (sometimes known in the United States as the 'graveyard shift') is the least liked and is often spoken of as unnatural, because it disturbs the 'diurnal rhythms of life' (body temperature tends to be highest in the afternoon and lowest in the early hours of the morning)". (p.17 Chapter 5, part 2).

A great interest is still taken in this field today. Simon Folkard (1987) has written an interesting article 'Circadian Rhythms and Hours of Work' which deals with body temperature at certain times of the day and the fact that sleep deprivation may actually impair productivity and safety in the working environment.

There is one area of investigation in fatigue study that was not considered before and that is the problem of 'man computer interaction' (Warr 1979). Clearly Oakley was not presented with this issue in his time. Of course, the introduction of new technology in the workplace will always have a significant impact on the study of occupational psychology. John Fox (1987) writes on 'Artificial Intelligence in the Workplace' and mentions how computer technology has had a tendency to deprive some workers of their jobs, yet at the same time is absolutely necessary for the progress of a firm.

ENVIRONMENTAL ENGINEERING:

Under this heading, Charles Oakley wrote about such topics as lighting, ventilation and heating, and noise control. He asked about this fairly regularly on exam papers. For example:

5. "If you have only a limited amount to spend on improving a factory's environmental conditions next year, what would be your first approach - by lighting, heating and ventilation or noise abatement?" (paper from 6th June 1969).

Compared to modern research on such phenomena, the concerns have remained more or less the same. Oakley wrote an interesting section on the importance of colour in firms for visibility (1962). He writes about how psychologists recommended tinted colours for factory decoration schemes -

such as pale versions of buff, slate grey or greyish green - in proference to white. He says that white reflects more of the light that falls upon it and that this can create disturbing glare effects and show up dirty marks. He explains how colours can also be used to increase the visibility of various items, such as switches, starting buttons and tool points. He says attention can be called to dangerous features - blue was known as the cautionary colour for electrical gear and orange was and still is used in connection with some hazardous operations. The only difference found in more recent research on colour in the working place is that there is more of an emphasis on the effect of colour on <u>behaviour</u> (Harris and Hartman 1992). These authors give a list of colours and their effects. For example, blue 'decreases breathing and pulse rate; causes tranquillity; but too much and rather dark shades of blue may cause depression'. Another example they give is that of light shades of most colours which' affect people's sense of time passage and makes time seem to pass faster. It is often used with monotonous jobs. (p.93).

PREVENTION OF ACCIDENTS (SAFETY ENGINEERING):
On this subject Oakley taught about psychological factors, such as levels of awareness and reflex actions, accident proneness, distraction, psycho-analytic theories (poorly adjusted people), and stupidity or perversity (people who take risks). Most of these headings are self-explanatory, whilst the last two are not at all that clear. For psycho-analytic theories, Oakley attempted to explain how some investigators

had taken a psycho-analytic line to study the link between emotional instability and accident frequency. In other words, 'emotionally unstable' people may get themselves involved in accident producing situations to cover up personal deficiencies, or to escape from personal difficulties, or to win sympathy, or perhaps just to attract attention to themselves (Oakley 1962).

By 'stupidity or perversity', Oakley was referring to the way in which 'the man who takes chances knowingly is often able to get away with it' (p.27 chapter 4 - ibid). In Oakley's view the misfortunes come to others of lesser skill who copy such a man; in other words, working speedily leads to fewer accidents than <u>trying</u> to work speedily. A question Oakley set for his students in light of these arguments was: 'Outline some of the theories that have been propounded about accident proneness'. (paper from 15th September, 1958).

Oakley's approach can be compared with the modern 'Personnel Selection Approach' for the reduction of accidents (Muchinsky 1993). This is about making predictions regarding the likelihood of certain individuals having accidents. Muchinsky points out that research on the value of personality tests to predict accidents has generally been disappointing. He mentions that such tests were used to assess a candidate's personality even when there was no established relationship between test scores and job success. For this reason, personality measures came under attack and were seen to be invading the privacy of the individual. The author discusses the development of new tests by industrial and occupational psychologists. He gives the example of Hogan, Hogan and Busch (1984). They created a personality scale designed to measure the ability to be helpful in dealing with other people, assessed by such factors as being thoughtful, considerate, and cooperative.

THE ART OF MANAGEMENT:

Under this heading, Oakley lectured on such topics as the Personnel Function in Management, the Changing Conception of Supervision, Selection and Training for Management, and Patterns of Leadership. These areas of study are now known as 'occupational social psychology' (Warr 1979). The main difference between Oakley's research and more recent research is the way in which leadership is studied. Oakley's work concentrated on the personal qualities of a leader, for example self-centred leaders who like having authority over others, have confidence in themselves and have no unsettling worries about rivals for their post, are trusted as well as liked, know their own mind and are decisive. (Oakley 1962 chapter 5). David Guest (1987) says that personal qualities of a leader were indeed the concern of earlier researchers. He believes that personal qualities are important for the success of leaders but that the context is at least as important. Guest says there is now more of a emphasis on the study of leader behaviour'. For example he looks at Likert's study on the impact of 'autocratic' versus 'democratic' styles of leadership.

VOCATIONAL GUIDANCE:

Charles Oakley looked at such factors as level of intelligence, scholastic attainments, special abilities and interests, and qualities of personality such as attainments in mathematics, science and manual crafts. Vocational Guidance does not seem to have much priority in more recent occupational psychology textbooks. It is quite clear that Oakley took a strong interest in vocational guidance because it was the primary concern of his work with the Scottish Division of the N.I.I.P. An interesting exam question Oakley set for his students was: "How would you give vocational guidance to university students (a) when entering and (b) when leaving the university?" (15th September 1958).

This is of course still relevant today, especially as there is an increasing percentage of the population now attending higher education.

Testing for vocational guidance and selection is different now because rather than being based on intelligence tests (e.g. verbal or arithmetic), students will now take what are called 'Interest Inventories' (McCormick, and Ilgen 1981). They give an example of one called Holland's Vocational Preference Inventory (VPI) which provides for scoring of interests in the following six categories: (R) Realistic; (I) Intellectual; (A) Artistic; (S) Social; (E) Enterprising; and (C) Conventional. Clearly, there has been a move away from purely intellectual tests to using such inventories as the VPI to assign occupations to different classifications consisting of 'combinations' of the above categories. The authors give the example of how advertising and salesmen are in a category designated ESC (Enterprising, Social, Conventional).

ACHIEVEMENT OF THE N.I.I.P. SCOTTISH DIVISION:

According to its Constitution, the objects of the Scottish Division were "to extend and encourage the practical application of Psychology and Physiology to commerce and industry in Scotland and to provide a local organisation for members of the Institute residing there." (minutes of N.I.I.P. Executive Committee 1933-37).

In some ways it had achieved its aim, but the Scottish Division did this indirectly through Vocational Guidance. According to a 1937 minute, Oakley reported that excellent progress was being made towards to the goal which they announced last year of having a careers master or mistress appointed in every Scottish Secondary School within ten years. He reported that 41 Vocational Guidance cases had been examined in Scotland during the year. The locations of cases are as follows:

Glasgow District	20
Edinburgh	5
Dundee	2
Renfrewshire	3
Borders	2
Perthshire District	2
Ayrshire District	3
England	4

Clearly Glasgow benefited the most - perhaps this was because the Divisions office was located there (at 142 St. Vincent

Street). In the same report, Oakley talks about the Industrial Development Work done by the Division. He describes how during the last 18 months most of the Division's work, apart from lectures and Vocational Guidance, had been related to industrial development. The Survey of Recent Scottish Industrial Developments was in progress and was to be published shortly by the Moray Press (Edinburgh).

Oakley commented on how the Industrial Map of Scotland was almost completed, but the need for a careful checking was to delay its publication until May. This is evidence that the Scottish Division did come out with published work, especially as a result of Oakley's talent and enthusiasm. Also, Oakley reported that during the year they had continued to contribute a monthly article to the Chamber of Commerce Journal, and were at that point writing the leading article of about 12,000 words, for the Chamber's Annual Special Number. They had also prepared the brochures for the new Scottish Industrial Estate. They were continuing to serve on several committees including the Exhibition Committee, the Scottish Economic Committee's Statistical Sub-Committee, and the Committee forming the Junior Chamber of Commerce. This is all evidence that the Division was very active in Scotland. It is also interesting that they wrote a monthly article in the Chamber of Commerce Journal, because it means that it was not just the London Division publishing material.

Another report on the Scottish Division's activities was the minute of the Seventh Annual General Meeting (1937). At this meeting, Oakley reviewed the work of the Division and mentioned that it had made considerable progress in one of its chief aims, the establishment of vocational guidance in Scotland. This helps confirm the assumption that most of the Division's work was in the area of vocational guidance. There was discussion of an important development when Mr. J. Morrison was appointed Supervisor of Investigations for Scotland and the North of England. He was attached to the Division's Office in Glasgow and was concerned primarily with Scottish investigations. This is an important detail, as there is not much known about who was doing the few Scottish investigations that were carried out.

The most interesting part of this report is that dealing with the Report and Accounts for the year to 30th September 1936. The Chairman (John Urie) referred to the Statement of Accounts and said it was comforting to see an increase in the fees from Lectures and Vocational Guidance and a substantial increase in Fees from Investigations. At the same time, he said it was disconcerting that the Division had not yet approached the stage of being self-supporting. As he pointed out, the Division was unfortunately dependent on donations and these were coming from a very limited number of individuals. He observed that the Division was at a point when an energetic campaign was required to establish the Division financially for a further period of activity. This of course was highly unlikely, as the London Division itself was heading for a difficult year in 1938 (see 'The Troubled 1930's in appendix).

Unfortunately, the Scottish Division folded in 1951. The minute from the 17th of May 1951 contains information as to why this happened. In the meeting, Dr. Frisby explained that for the Division to continue, it would be essential to have a full time Director. He mentioned that apart from the fact that Oakley was continuing in the Government Service and so not available to the Division on a full-time basis, the financial resources of the Division would not permit the employment of a full-time Director. This was probably because of what Oakley was talking about when he wrote that the management consultancy firms were taking all the assignments from the N.I.I.P. (see Oakley - background information). Frisby then suggested that the Scottish Division should be finally wound up and that a new Regional Committee should be formed to act in liaison with the National Institute in London in promoting in Scotland the objects of the Institute. Whether this committee was formed or not is not know. However, it was clear that the Institute in London was never really interested in the Scottish Division and this was why the Scottish Division had such a short life (1928 - 1951) while the London Institute remained active from 1921 - 1977.

CHARLES OAKLEY - BACKGROUND INFORMATION: (CONTINUED IN APPENDIX)

According to his autobiography, Charles Oakley was born at Portsmouth in 1901. He graduated from Glasgow University with Honours degrees in Mechanical Engineering and Naval Architecture. He says that he decided not to pursue his career in engineering and after a short spell in journalism (he specialised in cartoon drawing) he moved from Glasgow to Aberdeen to take up a post as Assistant Lecturer in Educational Psychology at Aberdeen University. After three years in Aberdeen, followed by a short stay in London, he returned to Glasgow and to the staff of the University there. He remained a member of this staff from 1930 - 1973, except for a spell of thirteen years during and after the Second World War when he was seconded to the Civil Service.

Oakley goes into more detail about this in his 1993 writings. He says he took up his duties with the N.I.I.P. in the Spring of 1930 having previously spent almost a year on the N.I.I.P. research staff in London. Again, he describes how he resigned from Aberdeen University to take that appointment which was to be preparatory to his returning to Glasgow University.

In Oakley's opinion, the first few years went well in spite of strains caused by the Depression. He mentions how in 1935 vocational guidance was recognised by the Scottish Education Department as a qualification for extra salary under Article 39, and thereafter an afternoon vacation course was run for three weeks each July in Moray House, Edinburgh, until the outbreak of war in 1939. In 1935 the Handbook of Vocational Guidance was written by Dr. Angus Macrae, later of the British Medical Association, and Oakley, and was published by the University of London Press.

From 1936 to 1939 Oakley says that classes continued to grow and requests for vocational guidance (for which a fee of three guineas was charged) grew steadily (He limited himself to 50 cases a year and in total must have dealt with between 400 and 500 cases during the decade).

After 1935 the newly-established management consultancy firms set up offices in Scotland. With their professional approach they took virtually all Scottish assignments away from the N.I.I.P. In the summer of 1936 Oakley intended to leave Scotland and become Director of the British Film Institute, but was persuaded at literally the last moment not to do so by Sir James Lithgow and Norman Duthie. While continuing the lectureship (by this time at the University, Royal Technical College, Paisley Technical College and Moray House) and vocational guidance, he gave up consultancy in industrial psychology and switched to Scottish industrial development, as an adviser to the newly appointed Scottish Economic Committee, and consultant to Sir James Lithgow's committee then trying to revive the Scottish aircraft industry. This led to Oakley's taking an active part in organising the 1938 Empire Exhibition, including preparing the book "Scottish Industry Today" for the Scottish Development Council, as well as the Industrial Map of Scotland and the Buyers guide also for that Council. In effect, although he did not realise it at the time, Oakley was being trained for the duties he was to undertake in the coming war. His book on industrial psychology, "Men at Work", was due for publication by the University of London Press at the end of 1939. It was held back and not published until late 1945 when it went through several editions, partly because the Fighting Services adopted it as reading matter for young officers before returning to civil life.

1939 - 1953: Shortly after the declaration of war Oakley was seconded by the University to take up an appointment as Scottish Area Officer in the Air Ministry, and subsequently became Scottish Controller (and for a period also North of Ireland Controller) for the Ministry of Aircraft Production. At the end of the war he was appointed Scottish Controller of the Board of Trade, still as a temporary civil servant.

In 1948 Oakley declined an invitation to become a permanent civil servant. This was done in consultation with Sir Hector Hetherington. The Board of Trade agreed to his giving evening lectures to the newly established course on industrial administration and so he believes "I am unique in having participated in every session since its formation almost 20 years ago". (p.2 - section 5a - 1993).

Charles Oakley remained the Board of Trade's Scottish Controller for several more years. In session 1951-52, however, one of the Professors of Engineering informed him that he would either have to resume his course of lectures to engineering students or make way for someone else. So at the end of 1952 he retired from the Board of Trade, after 13 years as an Assistant Secretary in the Civil Service, and resumed his lectures in October, 1953.

1953 - 1966: Several changes had taken place in the meantime.

(1) The fund responsible for Oakley's salary as a part-time lecturer had been wound up, and the University now accepted this responsibility (only John Drysdale of the founders was still alive).

(2) The N.I.I.P. had itself virtually given up consultancy (its activities having been greatly affected by the growth of the professional management consultancy firms). It had been converted into a research body receiving grants from government and other bodies. In 1948 it had dissolved its Scottish and other Divisions, and had renounced its interest in the lectureship at Glasgow University. This was done in consultation with Jack Mavor (Sam Mavor's nephew and his successor as head of Mavor and Coulson) and himself, and was eventually regarded as having been a mistake. Oakley comments: "Dr. C.B. Frisby, the Institute's Director, says that they did not believe that I really intended ever to leave the Civil Service to return to the University". (Section ..).

In this period, Oakley says the number of students had greatly increased - for instance, his engineering course, which had attracted about a dozen students each session before the war, now amounted to over eighty. He had to divide up other classes also and to give further courses to the management students. This lead to his giving in some sessions five lectures on Mondays and four on Fridays.

As Scottish Controller of the Board of Trade he had taken, at the suggestion of its President, Sir Stafford Cripps, an active part in the post-war years in forming the British Institute of Management and its Scottish Council, and this had brought him into close contact with the leading firms of management consultants. He now became adviser on industrial psychology to Urwick, Orr and Partners, and a director of E.G. Brisch and Partners. Oakley still held both these appointments, although not in the active sense of a few years ago. He travelled down South at mid week and not only was associated with developing Urwick Orr's College at Slough but lectured occasionally in each session to the engineering production students at Birmingham University.

During this time, Charles Oakley retained his personal contacts with the staff of the National Institute of Industrial Psychology and had been impressed from time to time when told of the development of industrial psychology (Oakley points out it was now being called 'occupational psychology') at various British universities, notably Cambridge and London. He observes how Scotland was still well ahead (Glasgow) in the total number of students taking industrial psychology courses each year.   He seemed to regret that they did nothing but lecture:

"As we are the oldest 'graduating lectureship' in Great Britain it seemed a pity that no research or other investigations were undertaken, but I could not see how, in view of my other commitments, this could be done. Indeed, the final manuscript of my successor to Men at Work, although often revised, has still to be handed over to the University of London Press".

DISCUSSION AND CONCLUSIONS:

The questions posed at the beginning of this paper have now been answered to an extent. However, it took a much longer time to arrive at them than at first anticipated. We have discovered that the Scottish Division probably survived for the short time it did because of Oakley's dedication to it. It was also interesting to find that Myers did not in fact choose Oakley for the position of Director of the Scottish Division and really didi not have much to do with setting it up. Oakley's Division never did receive the funding it needed, but still he managed several successes in vocational guidance and would have probably been consoled by the fact that his Division had achieved much in the area of Vocational Guidance, which was the original aim of the Scottish Divsion. It was unfortunate that the S.D.N.I.I.P. folded in 1951, but as was mentioned earlier, the relationship between Myers and Oakley certainly would not have facilitated such matters. Indeed, the Scottish Division might have survived if the London Division had 'given more attention to the commercial aspects' (Duncan).

Both Divisions can be said to have contributed to British Occupational Psychology. We have seen for example that much of what Oakley taught in his day is still relevant to headings found in more recent textbooks.

The above aspects of Oakley's life are interesting, although they do not form a picture of the man as a whole. Oakley's interests were widespread. He was into journalism (articles, especially cartoons), was into film and happpened to be a well known figure in Glasgow for his expertise in Industry and Commerce. I have catalogued some of his unpublished work, but only that which is relevant to my paper. C.A. Oakley's daughter is in possession of three times the amount of material I have catalogued. A future researcher could therefore write Oakley's Biography.

Finally, those interested in the history of Occupational Psychology should look more carefully at such organisations as the N.I.I.P. and S.D.N.I.I.P. because as was shown in this paper, these organisations played a crucial part in what was happening to the reputation of Industrial Psychology from the 1930's onwards.

-APPENDIX 1-

OAKLEY'S PUBLICATIONS
(works not mentioned in this paper)

Dear old Glasgow town. (1975) London, Blackie.

Handbook of vocational guidance: secondary and public schools. (1937) (By C.A. Oakley and Angus Macrae); preface by C.S. Myers. London: University of London Press.

The Second City. (1946) London: Blackie.

History of a Faculty. (1973) University of Glasgow, Faculty of Engineering Jubilee Committee.

The Fleeting Years- a collection of drawings of incidents and personalities at Glasgow University. (1951) Published by Glasgow University Graduates Association on the occasion of the Fifth Centenary celebrations.

Scottish Industry today; a survey of recent developments. (1937) Edinburgh, The Moray Press.

The Last Days of the Apprenticeship System (1943) Industrial Welfare, p.9.

The Industrial Misfit. (1934) Human Factor, vol.8.

Electric Welding: The Rise of a New Craft. (1933) Human Factor, vol. 7 pp. 312-317.

A New form Board. (1935) Human Factor, vol.9, pp. 105-108.

A First Survey of Psychological Testing in Secondary and other schools- I. (1935) Human Factor, vol.9 pp.138-146.

A First Survey of Psychological Testing in Secondary and other schools-II. (1935) Human Factor, vol.9 pp.186-200.

Our Illustrious Forebears. (1980) (about Glasgow) Blackie and Son Ltd., Glasgow.

Scottish Industry. (1953) Printed in U.K. by Collins Clear-Type Press.

Industrial map of Scotland; who's who and where of 2,500 industrial firms. (1939) Under the auspices of the Scottish Development Council and of the Scottish Economic Committee of the Scottish Development Council.

Scottish industry; an account of what Scotland makes and how she makes it. (1953) With a foreword by Lord Bisland.

FROM THE DAYS OF THE HORSELESS CARRIAGE.

in Glasgow it was decided to put up a notice to the effect that the book could be obtained from the Society on request.
Freshers' Tea. 34 new members had been enrolled.
The Metallurgist and Engineering, a lecture by J.W. Donaldson.
Visit by 50 members to **Dalmarnock Power Station**.
The Society's property was insured for £200.
Temperature Control by Oil Fuel, lecture by H.W. Ritchie.
The **first** award of the GUES Prize for 1932 was due to be awarded in January 1933.
Re proposed Association of members, there were about 2,000 members who could be circularised. It was agreed to allow about £10 for circularising. The book itself *(the year book)* would be published at the end of each summer vacation. A special committe was really necessary.
General Committee met on 22nd Feb.,1933, and recommended no visits between Xmas Vacation and Chanties day. GUES staged their show CANTEL at 255 Sauchiehall St., and decorated a lorry.
Visit to BBC Station at Falkirk.
GUES arranged for the **Faculty Engineering Photograph** to be taken, including first year men, so that the photograph need only be taken once every four years.
Year Book to be published. Next meeting was to be the AGM on March 10th, 1933. *(No minutes exist for this meeting.)*
Bonally Supper 4th April 1933, att. 85.

SESSION 1933-1934

The new President, C.A. Oakley, took the chair at the first **general committee meeting**. Messrs Oakley and G.G. McDonald were appointed to carry out the work in connection with the Year Book, with Mr Stein as Assistant Editor. Mr Dunlop Anderson reported that advertising agents in town would be willing to print the book free of charge in return for advertising space.
The approximate number of copies required was 2,500. The agents were not willing to pay postages, which with circularising would cost about £30.

"Ochre"

By May 4th 1933, the Year Book Circular was in the hands of the printer. Book to appear in September 1933, names of graduates being obtained from the General Council and checked by the Society's files.
It was recommended that only **four lectures and visits** be arranged. Functions were to include **Debate, Freshers' Tea, Smoker, Dance, Dinner and Bonally Supper.**
By 9th June, the Society had gifted a framed copy of the Faculty Photograph to the Department. Circulars for the Year Book had all been dispatched (2,400). The material for the next Year Book was well in hand. An appeal for Life Members was to appear in the Book.
By 21st Sep.,1933, the Year Book proofs were back in the hands of the publishers and issue was expected by the end of October. During preparation of the Book, Mr Dunlop Anderson's secretary had spent much of her own time typing the register and the manuscript. An Honorarium was suggested. It was suggested that a new card filing system be made for the future.
The **Bonally Supper** in the spring of 1933 had been attended by 85. It ended by the final year entertaining themselves in a story-telling competition.
The insurance value of GUES property was increased to £300.

Monday, 15th September, 1958

University of Glasgow

DEGREE OF BACHELOR OF SCIENCE IN ENGINEERING

INDUSTRIAL PSYCHOLOGY

(Not more than SEVEN questions to be attempted)

1. To what extent do you suppose that happy relations between factory managers and employees necessarily make for efficiency.
2. How would you give vocational guidance to university students (a) when entering, and (b) when leaving the university?
3. Write a short essay about the role of the instructor.
4. What are your views on the best length of the working week?
5. "Too much is being said about reducing factory noise and too little about washing factory windows." Discuss.
6. James Watt's workshop tools are said to bear a close resemblance to those in use in modern British workshops. Discuss from the standpoint of movement study.
7. What is the relationship between physical fatigue and the feeling of tiredness?
8. Outline some of the theories that have been propounded about accident proneness.
9. Do you think that greater or lesser use will be made of financial incentives in factories during the next twenty years?

WRITTEN BY C.A. OAKLEY

Friday, 6th June, 1969   9 a.m. to 12 noon

University of Glasgow

MASTER OF ADMINISTRATIVE STUDIES
IN MANAGEMENT (FIRST YEAR)
DIPLOMA IN MANAGEMENT STUDIES

BEHAVIOURAL STUDIES II

(Answer TWO questions from each section)

SECTION A

1. Persuasive managers are often disparaged as "men of words". Give your views.
2. Less use is made of vocational selection techniques in Great Britain than in most other Western European countries. Does this cause you concern?
3. What advice would you give the Engineering Training Board on using passing-out tests of competence?
4. Comment on the assertion that half the people off work today are quite capable of being back at work.
5. If you have only a limited amount to spend on improving a factory's environmental conditions next year, what would be your best approach - by lighting, heating and ventilation or noise abatement?
6. If asked to examine a factory's accident prevention arrangements, how would you proceed?

SOURCE → COLLECTION KEPT BY OAKLEY'S DAUGHTER.

CHAPTER V

John Dewar Cormack

Professor Cormack was elected GUES Honorary Vice-President for the year 1932-1933, and for the years 1934-1935 and 1935-1936. He made his mark more as an administrator and teacher rather than in experimental research. He was devoted to the University and his students, was one of the founders in 1893 of the GUES, and he associated himself with all student activities, whether educational, social or athletic, having himself been a noted rugby player and golfer in his younger days. For decades he saw to it that no classes were held on Wednesday afternoons in Engineering so that all students could have the chance to partake in athletic pursuits. His interests covered civil, mechanical and electrical engineering, and among the offices he held were President of the Institution of Engineers and Shipbuilders in Scotland, and Chairman of the Glasgow and West of Scotland Association of the Institution of Civil Engineers. He was lecturing until a day or two before his death on 30th Nov., 1935. He was suffering from diabetes.

The Cormack Professorship in Civil Engineering was founded in 1966, the first holder being H B Sutherland.

Minutes of the Society rarely mentioned the slump of 1930 to 1935, the disaster which afflicted the commercial world. Ochre's cartoon for the 1934 Bonally Supper, however, shows concern over employment prospects.

"Getting a job after graduation presented many difficulties."

SESSION 1931-1932

As no minutes remain of the proceedings at the AGM, the information has been extracted from reports of summer committee meetings. (I find it reported at the March 1937 AGM that the minute book was lost during that year.)

GLASGOW UNIVERSITY ENGINEERING SOCIETY BONALLY SUPPER

1934

Getting a job after graduation presented many difficulties. Shipyard foremen in these days wore Bowler hats (for protection from odd rivets dropping from above).

It was proposed to have a **lecture** on; **the work of a factory Inspector** by T.Brown; on **the new transmitting station for Scotland**, by N.Ashbridge of BBC; on **the human factor in industry** by C.A. Oakley; on **some aspects of Aeronautics**, by Sq. Leader G.F. Breeze; on **steel manufacture, rolling and fabrication**, by W.B. Scott of Redpath Brown & Co.

Four **visits** were proposed; to **Cardowan Colliery, Stephen & Sons' P & O Liner "Carthage", Glenfield & Kennedy** and **British Oxygen Co.**

A communication came in from P.W.Thomas, re publication of dates of meetings, etc. Seven arm chairs were on order for the Society Room.

CARTOONS DRAWN BY OAKLEY FOR THE STUDENTS (he called himself 'ochre').

Freshers' Tea. Mr Nithsdale was in the Chair. He expressed a hearty welcome to all first-year students and extolled the advantages of joining the Society. Two first year men were appointed to the committee. Att. 50.
52 members visited Cardowan Colliery.
Librarian reported sale of periodicals for 27/6. The Indian Union had requested the loan of the Society's tea service.

(A favourite cartoon with students). The Knight, a recent graduate in Thermodynamics, discovers that his text-book merely tells him what to do when encountering one-headed dragons.

The new transmitting Station for Scotland; lecture by N.Ashbridge of BBC, att. 80, of whom 20 came from the BBC.
Visit to P&O Liner "Carthage", att. 110.
P.W.Thomas (a graduate of 1922) was elected an Hon. Member at the **general meeting** on 19th Nov. He became secretary of the Federation of Engineering Societies in Glasgow. At one time GUES meetings were publicised in the Federation booklet, but as no 'technical' papers were published by GUES, Society meetings were omitted. The Year Book was not considered technical enough.
178 members had signed the membership book.
Extraordinary General Meeting to be called for 21st Jan., 1932. (This was attended by 15 members. It took place before the lecture by C.A. Oakley, when attendance was 45. An amendment to Constitution was adopted.)
Debate; Should one encourage boys to go in for Engineering?
Charity Day's "Black Hole of St Enoch's" had not been so successful this year. £75 collected as against £185. Notepaper sales had realised 5/5.
Service reminiscences in Aviation, lecture by Squ. Leader G.F. Breeze, att. 65.
On 29th March 1932, a proposal to grant a GUES prize was put before the Senate.
Attendance at **Bonally Supper** had been 63, a decrease of 44 from last year. *(No minutes exist for the AGM of spring 1932.)*

SESSION 1932-1933

On 9th June, 1932, the £5 GUES Prize was accepted for administration by the Senate. An inventory of the property of GUES was to be prepared for insurance purposes required by University Court.
On 22nd September, 1932, it was arranged that the GUES Prize for the most distinguished graduate of the year would be presented in the beginning of each year to that graduate appearing at the spring and autumn graduations of the preceding year.
Valuation of Society property was arranged. With respect to the booklet issued by the Federation of Engineering Societies

SOURCE: FROM THE DAYS OF THE HORSELESS CARRIA[GE] BY A.S. THOM.

A section of Oakley's 1993 writings.

CATALOGUE OF C.A. OAKLEY COLLECTION:

A. Oakley's teaching notebook:

1. Earliest exam paper dating 19th March 1931. Assorted papers dating up to 1956.

2. Class register for Oakley's course at Moray House from 1937-1938. This was a vocational guidance course for the National Committee for the Training of Teachers. (Oakley's handwriting-not typed).

3. Class register for Oakley's 1935 Summer School course for the National Committee for the Training of Teachers.

4. Paper: National Institute of Industrial Psychology Tests of Abilities and Other Qualities (Children over 11 years old). This is a list of Vocational Guidance Tests written by Oakley.

5. Poster announcing 'Two Free Public Lectures' on accidents which were to be given by Oakley on the 13th and 20th February 1935 in the Engineering Department.

6. Information on oakley's 13 lectures at Paisley Technical College, the Royal Technical College, and the Glasgow and West of Scotland Commercial College.

7. A list of books on Industrial Psychology- published by the Scottish Division: 1931-34.

8. Scottish Division Demonstration group tests no.'s 1,2,3,and 4.

9. A Report Form for Sales Assistants. (N.I.I.P.).

10. Report Form for Engineering Apprentices.

11. Poster for Oakley's five free public lectures on vocational testing in 1933.

12. Paper: The Selection of Employees. by Oakley (no date).

13. Paper: Industrial Investigations, written by Oakley for

the Scottish Division- no date.

14. <u>Paper:</u> The Selection of Young Workpeople by the Psychological Method. Written by Oakley for the Scottish Division- no date.

15. Class registers from Oakley's courses at Glasgow university.

<u>B.</u> Unpublished work by C.A. Oakley entitled <u>Industrial Psychology.</u> It was supposedly written after <u>Men at Work (1945)</u> in 1962. Chapters 1-6. Oakley based his lecture notes on this.

<u>C.</u> Folder containing various newspaper articles on Oakley, mainly published in the Glasgow Herald; various photographs of Oakley; proof of Oakley's success in journalism- an original draft of 'Spotlight on People and Places: Arbroath'. This was a kind of travel guide Oakley wrote in the Glasgow Bulletin (a newspaper which is now no longer active). Oakley wrote under the pseudonym- 'The Chiel'; Article: 'People I've known'. by Oakley. Not known which newspaper.

<u>D.</u> Loose exam papers dating from 1932-1971. Some papers were written for Heriot-Watt.

<u>E.</u> Notes on A4 paper in Oakley's handwriting about his experiences with the Scottish Film Council and famous people he met; article by Oakley about the 'Colquhoun' Dinner commemorating the 21st anniversary of the Junior Chamber of Commerce.

<u>F.</u> Envelope containing the original photos that were chosen for Oakley's autobiography; original cartoon drawings.

<u>G.</u> 'Proposed Occupational Psychology Unit at Glasgow University- Industrial Psychology at the University of Glasgow. (a note by Mr.C.A. Oakley)'.

<u>H.</u> Diary-style notes by oakley in his last year of life

(1993) - 26 pages.

Headings:

1. Back again to Glasgow.

2. How I came to be an Industrial Psychologist (lecturer on the subject 1930-1970); autobiographical information.

3. Skerry's helps me through.

4. I had to make my own way in the student's union.

5. How to write for the Newspapers.

6. My Bizarre First Day at the Institute.

7. My Three Meetings with Dr. Charles Myers.

8. Making Some Use of the University's Diploma.

9. 'Applied Common Sense'.

10. An Early Beginning to my Teaching Career.

11. 'Cheaper by the Dozen'.

12. Preparing my Lectures.

13. Work Study.

14. Three Years an Aberdonian.

15. The Handbook of Vocational Guidance.

16. Scotland's Best Student's Production.

17. Far from flourishing, as generally forecast the prospect's were....[undecipherable].

-APPENDIX 2-

D.D.- Yes, Charles Oakley was unusual in that he wasn't a Scot, he was an Englishman from Devon. But his Father was a Naval Architect, I believe, and so he wanted his son to follow in the business and he sent him to Glasgow to do an Apprenticeship. I'm not sure whether it was in Naval Architecture or as a Draftsman. While he was there he became interested...well one of the people that he contacted was a man called Mavor, of the firm of Mavor and Coulson.

L.A.- Yes, I found out that they sponsored the Engineering Department in Glasgow.

D.D.- That's right-yes. They also, I think sponsored him to take his degrees and you can find out from Glasgow University which degrees they were. I'm not sure whether his first degree was in psychology or not.

L.A.- Yes I did find a list of Oakley's qualifications which included his degree titles.

D.D.- So by the time he had qualified he decided that industrial psychology was what he wanted to be involved in. And so I think that after Mavor sponsored his Lectureship it was in the Engineering Department of the University. Now one of the implications of this is that for people who knew him and really valued what he had to teach, you almost have to look for the elderly graduate engineers from Glasgow University and I can name a few. Sir Monty Finiston who was very senior in British Steel was one of them and Sir Ian McGregor of the .... ?was another. If you approached the directors of G. and J. Weir in Cathecart I'm pretty sure their directors would know him. And so would people like Sir Eric Yarrow in Yarrow Shipbuilding. These are the ones I remember just now. But they are likely to have been his pupils and the accounts that I've had of him was that to the engineers this was a revelation. They had never thought of the human aspects. Now, his contact with N.I.I.P. was a central business of N.I.I.P. which was career or vocational guidance. And that was originated by Cyril Burt, Winifred Raphael continued it and there are quite a number of people in the 1930's carrying on vocational guidance. It never made much money. The profitable bits of the Institute's business were always the industrial investigations and problem solving in industry and they supported the vocational guidance side. Now Oakley got together with Angus Macrae and published Oakley and Macrae. Angus Macrae was a Scot, a qualified doctor was the secretary of the B.M.A. and would be about the same age as Charles Oakley and they published a book on vocational guidance. The other man was I think F.M. Earle and they did a study in Fife.

L.A.- Was that the study on Vocational Guidance in Fife?

D.D.- Yes. Fife was always something... in that region. I believe it was the Headmasters in Kirkaldy probably.

Now the lectureship in Industrial Psychology wasn't sufficient to make a living and so Charles Oakley rather took against what he regarded as the 'Cambridge Mafia'. You see, you had C.S.Myers who was a Cambridge Graduate. There was also Bartlett from Cambridge and there was that close link between Myers and Bartlett. The characteristic of all the Cambridge Graduates at that time was that they came from rich families. Oakley didn't come from a rich family.

L.A.- So why did Myers sponsor Oakley to work in the Scottish Division if they did not get along?

D.D.- Well, I don't know that they didn't get along. I think that there were other people who were at the head of the N.I.I.P. Myers was not a tremendously practical person and so he didn't much get involved with industrial investigations. There were other people who were responsible for developing that. Winifred Raphael was very active in this. And there was also a non-psychologist-a Director of N.I.I.P. who really was concerned with making money to keep it afloat. And one of the directors decided that it would be a good idea if there was a Scottish branch of the N.I.I.P. And so round about 1936 I think Oakley persuaded the N.I.I.P. to allow him to set one up.

L.A.-So you think it was Oakley that fired enthusiasm for a Scottish Division?

D.D.- Yes, I think it was Oakley who persuaded the N.I.I.P. to set up the Scottish branch. But he was very much an operator on his own. The people who came North found the Scottish climate rather different. It was heavily unionised. And if you look at the work that the N.I.I.P. did, it was very largely conducted in non-uninonised firms employing women, and Oakley on the other hand, was working very much in heavy engineeering in places employing men. Therefore, the people who came North didn't really fit that scene at all. And so Oakley kept very much to himself.

L.A.-Was he involved in any of the investigations?

D.D.- I don't think he got involved much in those activities at all. Seebohm Rowntree was one of the founders of the N.I.I.P. and he was a great supporter.

There is still a man alive in York called Bill Burges who was one of the last personnel directors of Rowntrees and he would be quite worth seeing, but you would probably find he hadn't much contact with Charles Oakley.

Meanwhile Charles Oakley built up support within Glasgow particularly and in shipbuilding and heavy engineering. That was really how he made his money up to World War II. With WW II he was made the Regional Director of the Board of Trade, which was really the government contact with industry applied side. That probably took him away from industrial psychology, although he was still always very much concerned with <u>being</u> an industrial psychologist. But I can tell you that I went to Glasgow in 1960, and I found the offices of I think, a printer and found a plate saying 'National Institute of Industrial Psychology-Scottish Division'.

I had a particular interest of course because as Regional Director of the Board of Trade Oakley was concerned quite a lot with preventing strikes in the heavy industry around Glasgow. So he was doing this after working for the government, but working really in industrial psychology. And in 1947 he published a book called <u>Men at Work</u>- University of London. One of the interesting points about that was that quite a bit of it was about women at work. Also, he was a person who promoted music while you work (in the book) for people working monotonous jobs in factories.

To me, his important feature was that ...I was in the RAF at a time when morale was very low and they were having mutinies which were being very carefully kept out of the papers. But it's simply because the R.A.F. suddenly didn't need any more air crew and they wouldn't release them. Instead of that, they were short of clerks. So they turned all the pilots and navigators into clerks and reduced them to the ranks. The officers tried hard to establish discipline and found it was impossible because the morale was so low. I hadn't read any psychology up to then but I was intrigued by this phenomenon of 'morale' and so I proceeded to look around the camp library for the people who wrote about morale and I found there were two. One was Charles Oakley's <u>Men at Work</u> which dealt with morale and the other was Norman Myers' <u>Psychology in Industry</u>. And from that point, Charles Oakley was someone I looked out for. When I went to Glasgow in 1960 I got to know him quite well. The other thing he wrote was <u>The Second</u>

City. Quite a lot of his money came from journalism, because The Second City was made up of articles which he published in the Evening Paper. Also, because of his activities as Director of the Regional Board of Trade he greatly encouraged the Glasgow Junior Chamber of Commerce.

L.A.- Yes, I checked with them and they had no information

D.D.- I see- but then your access to something like this would be individuals who were Seniors within the Chamber of Commerce who knew Oakley as involved in the Junior Chamber. I would say there's a chap called Ford Macpherson -I think he's a counselor now and it would be useful to get his views on Oakley.

Charles oakley had the reputation of being a tremendous after-dinner speaker and he was also reckoned to be the only man in Glasgow who could cope with two dinners in one evening!

L.A.-Which dinners are you referring to?

D.D.- He founded a series of Annual Dinners, called the 'Colqhoudon' dinners and these were sponsored by the Junior Chamber of Commerce but they were always very important occasions. I worked in Glasgow from 1960-65 on the Senior Executive Selection and so I came across quite a lot of the Senior people in industry in Glasgow and a lot of my very good contacts were made in the Junior Chamber of Commerce. There was an unusual mix of stockbrokers, business people, accountants, and commercial people. The Junior Chamber was where the professions got together with the manufacturing people. Charles Oakley was quite a notable figure in that area. He also wrote The Regional Guide to Glasgow. It was a full-colour illustrated guide to Glasgow.

L.A.- I find it surprising how little information Glasgow has on him if that was the case. At one point he was even called 'Mr.Glasgow'.

D.D.- I think it must be because he spread his activities fairly wide. He was involved in all sorts of things.

L.A.- I understand he was also involved in film.

D.D.- Oh yes-he was the founder of the Scottish Film society and was very active in that. He also founded a company called Jean McGregor's Soups!

L.A.- Yes, I was told that by Norman Maccallum of Glasgow University.

D.D.- Well, we had the common connection of course of the N.I.I.P. and he regarded me as a 'civilised Scot'. I thought quite a bit of him duriing that period

1960-65. He meanwhile would have liked me to take over his Lectureship. But that would have meant I would have had to abandon my career down South and really set up as a consultant in Glasgow and the timing was wrong for that.

The other thing was in terms of Glasgow's Universities-Glasgow University was of course the oldest. Then there was what was originally the Royal College of Science and Technology which became Strathclyde University. But Oakley was instrumental in founding the Glasgow and West of Scotland Commercial College which is now Glasgow's Third University. I think at the time of his death or certainly in his 80's, he was the Principal of that College and you might find out more from them.

L.A.- Do you have any idea why I was told that the Psychology department at Glasgow University did not really appreciate Oakley?

D.D.- Well you see there's a strange division in Psychology in Britain. The University departments were always trying to be more and more 'pure' psychologists, and the gulf between them and the Applied Psychologists was always quite considerable. I was five years with the N.I.I.P. (1953-58). They were striving for respectability in the eyes of academics and never quite achieving it. Their international reputation was very much higher than their British reputation. They were active in the International Confederation of Applied Psychology-I.C.A.P. And so we had quite a lot of International contact. Mrs.Gilbreth visited us once because Dr.Isabel Blain was one of her pupils.

The same thing I think happened in Glasgow. Because Oakley was in the Engineering Department, he could pursue just whatever he liked. But the result was that he was almost completely cut off from the staff of the Psychology department.

L.A.- Yes, Professor Maccallum was of the same opinion.

D.D.- Yes, that professor wouldn't be able to evaluate Oakley as a psychologist. There's no doubt that if you took Management Selection Ltd. in Glasgow, that was established in 1959 by Jim Smith who was a psychologist. I found from the start that because of Charles Oakley I was very much better understood as an Applied Psychologist in industry by the Engineering business than was the case in the South. In the South, they were very bashful about psychologists in industry, particularly in the Unions-any Unionised business. But in Scotland, the Unions seemed to know-and I would attribute this to Oakley because he taught the Engineering or Union bosses. The other place where you might go- have you tried the newspapers?

L.A.- No.

D.D.- The Glasgow Herald? It could be worthwhile. There could be some cartoons,etc.

L.A.- Well I have samples of cartoons he did for the students of Glasgow university.

D.D.- Oh- that was another thing you'll find. You know, there are two student songbooks he wrote and he was one of the editorial committee.

L.A,- Yes, I've come across those.

D.D.- But yes- I'm in no doubt about his contribution. Have you been in touch with Oastler Michie? Oastler was one of the psychologists who built up M.S.L. in Glasgow. There were five of us. Jim Smith went to London to be Managing Director, Wallace McMillan went to Manchester to be Head of the Manchester Branch of M.S.L. I went to Dublin to run management selection in Ireland and Oastler Michie became the Manager of Glasgow and he spent his career in Glasgow. He would have an observer's view of Charles Oakley. Have you been in touch with Tom Caruthers?

L.A.- It has been very difficult as he is only there part-time.

D.D.- Again, as an Applied Psychologist he would be useful as he applied psychology in industry. Charles Oakley gave a very interesting retiring address- I think when he retired as Principal of the Glasgow College and he sent me a copy which I have not been able to find. But that was largely autobiographical and I think he was fairly sensitive about the Southern Cambridge Graduates.

L.A.- What about the Institute's general reputation- putting Oakley aside for a moment?

D.D.- Well, among the firms you might say the firms that were conscious of human resources, their reputation was quite high. It was pretty well the one Institute which was concerned with the application of psychology to industrial problems. In 1958 I carried out a validation of their Apprentice Battery and there were some 30 firms which had installed it and had been operating it for the previous ten years or so and they were all very much in favor of it. The Institute came to an end around 1972 or so and it was this search for 'purity' which defeated them, because they had a number of real commercial winners which they didn't follow up.

I was trained in marketing before I joined the Institute and I always thought of marketing strategies and this was regarded with horror, but the Institute was a non-profit making business. So they didn't realise that they had to make profits somewhere. And they got more and more 'introverted' as the years went on. The one really profitable side of the business was running courses in the use of psychological tests for non-psychologists. I did a lot of that.

L.A.- So is it true that the Institute just went bankrupt?

D.D.- In a way, yes. Dick Buzzard was really a very nice, very hospitable man, but not commercially minded at all. Really he forfeited the trust of the people who were financing his research and neglected the commercial side of things. But I've always found that they had a very consistent clinical philosophy.

About five years ago I organised a reunion of N.I.I.P. people and there was a real network- and this was twenty years after. All these people were talking the same language and getting on well together. There were about 40 or 50 of us. We had to deal with the argument that you shouldn't be teaching non-psychologists to use tests. What they didn't see was that there was a demand for tests to be used and it had to be controlled and developed by the Institute. In 1971 there was a Jubilee edition. Have you come across that?

L.A.- Yes. I've also gone to L.S.E. and found minutes of the Scottish Division meetings.

D.D.- Really? What were the names- who was attending?

L.A.- There was John Urie as chairman.

D.D.- Urie... Now he's a Scottish businessman I think rather than a psychologist.

L.A.- There was also Stevenson.

D.D.- Arthur Stevenson? Yes. Oh now that was another connection. Mr.Erwick formed a consultancy called Erwick Orr and Arthur Stevenson was a consultant there. Charles Oakley had the use of the office and the secretary of Erwick Orr and he was their advisor on psychological problems whenever they hit a problem where human resource knowledge was necessary. The secretary of Erwick Orr was the person who typed Charles' books. I could probably tell you more if I knew the people who were on that Scottish Division Board.

L.A.- I do have one of their meetings here, if you

want to take a look at it.

D.D.- You know of course that the N.I.I.P. developed the Black Magic Box of chocolates?

L.A.- Yes, I wrote about it. This meeting here is about what the English division thought Oakley should be responsible for.

D.D.- I see- oh, so John Mann was an accountant, and was the secretary. I knew his son. Yes- (reads it) so this really was the very first thing.

L.A.- I have about 30 more pages of these meetings but the L.S.E. apparently lost some of them.

D.D.- I made considerable efforts to keep the Institute afloat when it was plain it was going to fold. Only, they did not want to have commercial concerns running the Institute. But of course N.F.E.R. Nelson in effect owned the remnants of N.I.I.P. and the N.I.I.P. is not liquidated. if you refer to N.F.E.R. they will tell you they still have Annual General Meetings of N.I.I.P.

Yes, you see Oakley would be concerned with running investigations in Scotland and the question of Academic purity was being raised (in the meeting). And he succeeded in getting his support from the University?

L.A.- Yes.

D.D.- Duthie I think was an accountant-yes this is interesting. Welch was one of the people who supported Oakley (looking at my notes).

I'll give you the detail of the Black Magic Deal because when I left N.I.I.P. I went into consumer research and I did the product-testing for the 'Good News' assortment. I referred to the N.I.I.P. files. Nigel Balchin was an N.I.I.P. employee when they designed the Black Magic. And a man called Alec McBean thought up the name. He was a painter and a jazz enthusiast and he got the name from the song by the 'Inkspots' called 'That Old Black Magic'. That was the inspiration for the name. Alec Rodger was involved in the development as was Winifred Raphael.

The moment it was launched, Cadbury's suggested: 'And now you'll do one for us too?' So they all took a fright!! Instead of saying, we'll do these as independent investigations they brought into the Institute a Constitution that advised against being involved in Consumer Research. It immediately killed off a whole area in which psychology could very usefully have been applied. And that was in 1933 when they needed all the money they could get. Again, when I left N.I.I.P. I went to work for a company called

'Atwood Statistics'. Atwood statistics was formed by a man called Bedford Atwood who in 1933 was working for J.Walter Thomson who had the Rowntree's account and who involved N.I.I.P. in the product-testing of the assortment. Thomson was the company that J.B. Watson went to work for when he was fired from his University post.

    L.A.- Could you tell me what you think about the N.I.I.P.'s wider influence on industrial psychology? That is what's missing from what I've written so far.

    D.D.- You've probanly seen my paper that I gave to Dave Fryer?

    L.A.- Yes.

    D.D.- Yes, well it's very interesting... I was reading a book by David Canter called <u>Criminal Shadows</u> which is about criminal serial killers and he describes quite graphically what I would call the 'inside-out' approach to analysing people. He mentioned that he studied under Hearnshaw at Liverpool University. Now Hearnshaw was an investigator at N.I.I.P. from 1933-1938 and the approach was to quite an extent 'behaviourist', in that you studied the environment at work but you then got down to considering the people in that environment. And you built up the story from that, but you always asked the people what they thought of the work they were doing. Winifred Raphael in particular pioneered what we call 'attitude surveys' and this was when the top man in a company would say "There's something wrong with this company and I don't know what it is." And the Institute would go in and interview a sample of people. The Director met them, recorded it on punch cards and would then analyse it and we would come out with a list of suggestions which recommended what they ought to do and we insisted that they did implement it. This was a very successful technique, and when I got involved in consumer research I found this was exactly what was done in consumer studies. They had both the quantitative techniques and the qualitative techniques. But it was very difficult for anyone in the Institute to get anything published. Clifford Frisby was a ferocious man for that.

    You see, I know that if I find someone who has been involoved with the Institute I know they'll have the same approach as I do. It's basically an 'atomistic' approach, that is, you are dealing with the individual at an individual level. You are observing as far as possible, but all the time his or her view of the work situation. The way in which skilled operators <u>perceive</u> their work is also important. But you are never in a position to do a proper laboratory experiment, because you cannot have algorithms and something always happens to wile it up.

I did get involved in one long investigation. The police cars... when they made tires with tubes in them there were a few deaths among the police, because the tires would blow out at a certain speed and they decided that something was wrong with their tires. So I was asked to investigate. I went in and the first thing I noticed was the inspectors were inspecting by the factory light which was fairly dim. I then instituted a marking system whereby each inspector's work could be identified and I brought the factory to a standstill for four hours, but in the four hours I was able to prove that each inspector had his own idea about what the fault was, they each had their own fault specialty and I subsequently discovered that they didn't know what they were looking for. I also discovered that their eyesight was defective, because the oldest men were always put on inspection (once they were over 45). Also, I found that insufficient time elapsed, from the time that the tires came out of the mould- and they said 'but it's not visual, it's tactual'. I discovered that the tires were too hot to handle. I suggested that they ought to develop something powered by an electric motor, which would have two rollers which would rotate the tire and to this fixture could be attached a light which would shine on the inside of the tire and this would relieve the inspector of the weight of handling it and so on.

L.A.- Did they follow your suggestions?

D.D.- Two years later they did! I had also installed a training course in which I found 50 tires with all the known faults and I used this as a test first of all on the inspectors to prove they hadn't a clue what they were looking for! But I also used it as a training device so that they <u>did</u> know what they were looking for! And that I believe solved the problem. It was simple common sense, but it worked. One of the questions which was always being asked was 'What's your evidence? If you made a statement in the Institute, you always had to be prepared to provide your evidence for it. No-one got away with wild theories. Again with interviewing, we taught people how to assess personality. The idea was that the interview was to be used to improve selection- An objective, thorough interview.

L.A.- I was reading that Winifred Raphael did some work on interviewing technique.

D.D.- Oh yes- that's right. She was a very good interviewer. But it was basically the Carl Rodgers 'Non-Directive' approach which she applied. Also job specifications... they were real pioneers in specifying what jobs required, so that you knew what you were trying to fill. Of course once again the M.S.L. was founded on the one hand by Alec Rodger who was an industrial psychologist and by Harry Ross who had been trained by Winifred Raphael. In fact Winifred had trained all the Directors. So the N.I.I.P. was fundamental in training the consultants in executive selection in the U.K. I had quite a number of them on my courses, from the major consultancy companies. I did quite a number of book reviews. You'll find them in 'Occupational Psychology' between 1956-1958. Whenever I got furious at the frustrations I experienced in the Institute, I used to write a review, and the reviews were full of points which I thought the Director ought to take up- to my amazement, he used to love them. I didn't get many things published, because my orientation was far too commercial.

L.A.- Was that not the case with most of the members of the Institute?

D.D.- Yes. They left because they could see that lots of commercial opportunites were being wasted. And a lot of them were quite successful in industry and commerce after that, upon leaving.

L.A.- What about Oakley's involvement in industry and commerce? I believe he was involved in a project for Rolls Royce in Glasgow.

D.D.- Yes- Hillington. I think it was the aero-engine. That was plagued with strikes and we installed a test battery there- 'the Apprentice Test Battery'. For every 10 apprentices applying, maybe one would be taken on and they found that the Unions and Management were not very good at selection, and so they adopted testing as a way of improving this. The one effect was that a lot of them went straight up into Senior Management and missed out... it wasn't so much of a contribution to good shop-floor workers as providing good middle-management.

L.A.- Could you possibly give me an idea of the general atmosphere in the U.K. at the time?

D.D.- Well, at the time I was working at the N.I.I.P., there was full employment.

L.A.- Was the N.I.I.P. concerned with matters of unemployment?

D.D.- Well they were concerned with 'Misfits'. That is, they did quite a lot with vocational guidance you see, implying that if they made the right choices they could have a good career. But if people didn't know enough, they made the wrong choices. Some examples- If you read Ludovic Kennedy's autobiography On the Way to the Club . He was advised by the N.I.I.P. that he should not try to be a novelist, as he wasn't creative enough. The interesting point was that his talents have been as an investigator of facts- a crime writer. So that was good advice. Another example was Sir Anthony Part who was in the civil service and was successful because of vocational guidance.

When I came back from Dublin to London with M.S.L. it was to set up a psychological section within M.S.L. and this included some counseling, and one of the people I counseled was a chap who had just taken a brilliant first class honours degree from L.S.E. and all his lecturers had been saying 'You have a brilliant academic career in front of you- you really should go on'. He wasn't too happy about this and so I put him through one of my tests and discovered that one of the options he had was to join his brother in advertising. His name was Morris Satchie. So the trouble with that is that you have so many individual cases which are very successful but it is clinical validation rather than statistical validation. Anyway, this thorough approach of using tests to get an accurate picture of a person at the point of turning... you always consider the background right from the start. In other words- what a person has done in the past, they will do in the future. That was really what we were taught at the Institute. We were taught to be thorough and objective as far as possible. So it really was a great pity that it could no longer go on. But with more attention to the commercial aspects it could have been a great success.

L.A.- Do you know what went on when the N.I.I.P. was first set up?

D.D.- 1921? That was the Australian Muscio who worked in this country. The people at the end of the War became very interested in industrial administration. Myers got this idea of an Institute from Muscio. And Cyril Burt and Raphael were also active in the formation of this. You see Myers himself was not a commercial animal at all and you'll find that he depended on businessmen like Welch and Miles to point the Institute in a direction so that it would be able to make profits.

L.A.- It still isn't quite clear to me why Myers was interested in setting up a Scottish Division.

D.D.- I think it was far more an initiative of Charles Oakley. And that minute implied that they were a bit doubtful about Charles and his ability to carry out an investigation unsupervised. And so I think it was the pressure from him. The Scottish Division was very much Charles Oakley's foundation and essentially, once he had established it, they just left him alone!

L.A.- I wish I could have found some kind of a commentary relating to this issue.

D.D.- One of the really dreadful things was that when the Institute folded, Dick Buzzard took the view that the Records were confidential and so destroyed all the industrial reports.

L.A.- Around what date did this happen?

D.D.- That was 1972 or 1973. That's probably the sort of scientific advisory committee meetings- that sort of thing(when L.A. mentioned a file was closed in L.S.E.). The view was taken that reports were confidential if the companies had commissioned them. It was a pity because a lot of useful work had been destroyed. Some of the tests developed by the Institute are now in the Science Museum.

L.A.- Yes I went to see Tim Boon but he still has no catalog. I saw two tests on display. There was a biscuit packer's test and a manual dexterity test on display.

D.D.- Yes that will be what we called the R.V. manual- R for Rodger and V for Vincent. That will be the one in which you drop ball bearings into a tube?

L.A.- Yes.

D.D.- That was originally part of the Apprentice Selection Battery and it had very poor reliability, because if people were at all nervous they would drop the ball-bearings! It was very liable to nervousness. I can tell you what the Apprentice Battery was, because I installed a number of these. They had Group test 70 which was non-verbal, and group test 33 which was a verbal test. They had two-dimensional spatial tests and they had something called 'Vincent Mechanical Models', which was succeeded by a thing called 'Vincent Mechanical Diagrams' which was a mechanical aptitude test. They had a ten-minute Arithmetic test, an Engineering information test (again ten minutes). They also used what we called the 'Elder brother's' test. This consisted of assembling various things for example a bulldog clip, etc. and because you could describe all these, younger brothers who were going through the apprentice battery always got a better score because their older brothers told them exactly what it was about!

L.A.- I came across a 'form board' by Oakley

D.D.- Oh yes- they had a number of these. That was for vocational guidance. We also used Sydney Crown's word association tests. We used T.A.T. as well- the Thematic Aperception test. I used to give the adult career guidance tests.

L.A.- You do know about the Handbook of Vocational Guidance?

D.D.- Yes, Oakley wrote most of that book and it sold very well, particularly in Scotland.

L.A.- ... I have some meetings here in which the Scottish Division is praising Oakley for his work. Would you mind looking at them?

D.D.- Well, R.H. Thoules was a psychologist and professor at Oxford, is the author of Straight and Crooked thinking and a book on general and social psychology. Stevenson was an N.I.I.P. investigator who later joined Urwick Orr. Norman Duthie was an accountant. Drysdale I think you'll find was a Scottish businessman. Now this was 1936.... so Oakley was appreciated in by the Scottish Division, but essentially, he was making his money elsewhere.

L.A.- I also have a list of Oakley's publications here.

D.D.- (looks at Oakley's article on accident prevention). Yes... you see, working in heavy industry, he was in the area where accidents most often happen. And so he had much more experience of accident prevention than one would get in the South.

L.A.- Oakley's papers 'The Industrial Misfit' and 'Psychological Problems of a Depressed Area' are also very interesting.

D.D.- The Institute were not tremendously exercised on behalf of the unemployed. Charles Oakley was in a depressed area and industries were depressed. In the South they were concerned with the developing industries- employing women, etc. These were the least affected by the depression. There was really a difference in atmosphere and a difference in emphasis.

-BIBLIOGRAPHY-

Frisby, C. (1970) The Development of Industrial Psychology at the N.I.I.P. Occupational Psychology, 44, p.35.

Harris, O.J. and Hartman, S.J. (1992) Human Behaviour at Work. West Publishing Company; New York.

Journal of the N.I.I.P. (1922) Copy available from British Psychological Society Archives.

McCormick, E.J., and Ilgen, D. (1981) Industrial Psychology. George Allen & Unwin; London.

Minutes from the meetings of the Scottish Division of the National Institute of industrial Psychology: 1929-1951.

Muchinsky, P.M. (1993) Psychology Applied to Work. Brooks/Cole Publishing Company, Pacific Grove.

Munsterburg, H. (1913) Psychology and Industrial Efficiency. Houghton and Mifflin; Boston.

Muscio, B. (1917) Lectures on Industrial Psychology.

Myers, C.S. (1942) Personal Record (a short autobiography held by the Royal Society).

Myers, C.S. (1925) Industrial Psychology in Great Britain. London: J. Cape.

Myers, C.S., Welch, H.J. (1932) Ten Years of Industrial Psychology. London: Pitman & Sons.

Oakley, C.A. (1983) Those were the Years- an autobiography. Blackie and Sons ltd., Glasgow.

Oakley, C.A. (1945) Men at Work. London: Hodder and Stoughton, University of London Press.

Oakley, C.A. (1962) the Last Tram. Written for Glasgow Corporation Transport Department at the closing of the tramways system, 4th September.

Oakley, C.A. (1951) Buyers' guide to Scottish industries; who's who and where of 5,500 manufacturing firms. (prepared for the Scottish Council).

Oakley, C.A. (1942) Accident Prevention in Industry. Occupational Psychology, vol.16, pp.111-119.

Oakley, C.A. (1940) Psychological Factors in Accident Causation. Occupational Psychology. vol.14, pp.181-183.

Oakley, C.A. (1936) Some Psychological Problems of a Depressed Area. Human Factor., vol.10, pp.393-404.

Oakley, C.A. (1962) *Industrial Psychology.* University of Glasgow. (unpublished).

Oakley, C.A. (1993) *Unpublished autobiographical notes in diary form.* Sections referred to: (1) How I came to be an Industrial Psychologist (used for Oakley's background information in Appendix).(2) My Bizarre First Day at the Institute (3) My Three Meetings with Dr. Charles Myers (4) Preparing my lectures.

Rose, M. (1975) *Industrial Behaviour.* Penguin Books, London.

Shimmin, S., and Wallis, D. (1994) *Fifty Years of Occupational Psychology in Britain.* Leicester: Division and Section of Occupational Psychology, British Psychological Society.

Thom, A.S. (1991) *From the days of the horseless carriage.* Published for the Centenary of Glasgow University Engineering Society by Glasgow University Engineers' Society. (Professor R.I. Maccallum of the Engineering Department at Glasgow University was kind enough to give me this book).

Warr, P. (1979) The content of journals relevant to industrial and organizational psychology (editorial). *Journal of Occupational Psychology,* 52, pp. 235-240.

Warr, P. (1987) *Psychology at Work.* Penguin Books; Middlesex. (articles used- Simon Folkard, John Fox, David Guest).

THE WORK OF THE N.I.P. 1921-1973

Throughout its life the N.I.I.P. published its own <u>Journal</u>. This was called <u>The Journal of the N.I.I.P.</u> (1922-1931), <u>The Human Factor</u> (1932-1937) and <u>Occupational Psychology</u> (1938-1973). The information on Myers' Institute in this paper comes from the <u>Annual Reports of the N.I.I.P.</u> which can be found at The London School of Economics and Political Science.

www.ingramcontent.com/pod-product-compliance
Lightning Source LLC
Chambersburg PA
CBHW042039240426
43667CB00040B/44